Do You Remember? - Dementia : Poetry from all perspectives.

Christina Kinney

BookLeaf Publishing

Presentation by *BookLeaf Publishing*

Web: www.bookleafpub.com

E-mail: info@bookleafpub.com

ISBN: 9789358737578

First edition 2024

*With complete respect, admiration and empathy
I dedicate this book in its entirety to all
Dementia survivors, loved ones, carers, medical
professionals and advocates*

*I offer special recognition to my gran Mrs
Helen Kinney, and all the residents I've cared
for within my work environment.*

*I hope to be the voice for those unable to
express it for themselves, and portray the
emotional whirlwind they encounter each day.*

*I honour the strength and bravery shown by
Dementia warriors, and will continue to make
sure their stories live on through words and
stories reflecting the journey they face.*

ACKNOWLEDGEMENT

For all who have faced, lived, survived, cared for, been involved in, or had any role in Dementia I thank you for inspiring this book.

Writing a book is an extremely spiritual, emotionally fulfilling and enjoyable experience, however, it can be very emotionally challenging.

I would like to thank all those I've encountered that have lived with Dementia for allowing me to learn from them and support them.

I would also like to thank all loved ones, family, friends, professionals, caregivers, and researchers/publishers for love, support, knowledge and dedication towards providing the best possible quality of life for Dementia patients.

Finally, I would like to thank BookLeaf Publishing for allowing this book to be published.

Most importantly however I'd like to thank every reader, supporter, or fan of this book, as without you sharing this story wouldn't be possible!

PREFACE

Dear un-dearest Dementia,

I write regretfully to you in agonising despair for all the pain you have caused, for all the loss and suffering, for capturing the ones that we love most. I feel it only fair to show the harsh reality behind the darkest parts of yourself that you imbed within our loved ones and each of our individual lives. It's important to share the trauma that it bares, so people can speak out and connect in the journeys they share.

Although there are still good times, and new memories you make that forever will stay, this book shares the emotional rollercoaster that all involved can compare and relate

I May Have Forgotten

Chapter 1: Can You Hear Me? - A Dementia Patient's View

I may have forgotten the names I called my kids, but I still remember holding their bottles when they were babies.

I may have forgotten the number one, but I know at eight in the morning my day has begun.

I may have forgotten what the words you speak mean, but I still remember phrases, things I hold dearly.

I may have forgotten the things that once made me full of life, but I still need stimulation, a little fun in my life.

I may have forgotten my manners, actions, or the words I speak, but I still think nothing's changed with me.

I may have forgotten how to engage in talking, interacting, or group activities, but I still get good days better than the bad, as everyone does naturally.

I may have forgotten how to show expressions
or emotions, but still want to hear from you, that
you love me and you're proud.

I may have forgotten all of myself, and who I
used to be, but this is who I am now, graciously
accept it and continue to love me the same way.

Do You Hear Me?

Chapter 1: Do You Hear Me? - A Dementia Patient's View

When you talk and I don't answer,
Do you still hear me?
Do you hear me?

When you look at me lovingly, and say I look
blank and numb,
Do you still read me as you did before?
Do you hear me?
Do you see me?

When you hug, kiss, and touch me, and I don't
move or ever do it back,
Do you still feel the warmth inside me?
Do you hear me?
Do you feel what's really inside me?

When I start to lash out, become aggressive, and
lose control, you stand static in shock, utterly
confused about how to calm me down or make
me stop.

Do you know it's genuinely nothing personal,
it's something I can't quite control,

Do you hear me?
Do you hear the pain and confusion I am in?

When I suddenly change and deteriorate fast,
I become a completely different person than the
one you always knew and loved.

Do you remember that inside I'm still the same
old me?
Do you hear me?
Do you hear all my thoughts, the old and new
me?

When I'm at the final stage of my life and
Dementia journey,
Will you remember to respect my previous
requests and wishes,
Incorporating my new ones If I request them?

Do you see me?
Do you hear me?

When all that's left is silence, and there's
nothing left to say.

Do you hear me?
Do you hear me?

Will you hear me and remember my words,
when I'm away?

If I Am…

Chapter 1: Can You Hear Me? - A Dementia Patient's View

If I am confused, using words wrong, not making sense, struggling to speak,
Please be patient, try to make sense of it, and help me condense.
Advocate my voice for me. Speak up loud and clear,
If I am a Dementia patient, let it proudly be known and fought deep.

If I am repetitive and forgetful,
Consistently going over the same things,
Please end the conversation lightly,
It's still the first time we've spoken to me.

If I am restless, overstimulated and can't sit down,
Don't tell me to sit quietly, or try to stop me from moving each time,
Walk with me, keep me safe and let my mind wander,
Grant me independence and that simple walk could be a new favourite memory.
If I am emotionally overwhelmed,

Upset, angry, loud, unable to be settled and
calmed down.
Give me space, comfort me, empathise,
Is it pain, is it fear, is it scary thoughts in my
mind?

If I am completely silent, or sometimes seem
more tired or down,
Remember I'm only human, I just more easily
burn right out.

If I am unaware, living my own version of
reality,
Don't correct me, or think who I was before I
changed,
If I am this now, then this is now me.

What Happened?

Chapter 1: Can You Hear Me? - A Dementia Patient's View

It started off slow and seemed so insignificantly small,
I refused to admit Dementia became part of me so largely,
So quick.

Information overload.

Medications and treatments aggressively collide.

Everything suddenly moving so fast,

Unable to process my thoughts, feelings and facts.

No time left to spare.

My only real memories being clinical, and action-based,

The tests, the diagnosis, the treatments, the endless involved services,

even legal work and major decisions thrown
instantly my way.

Overwhelmed. Actively tired. My brain in
overload.

Everything already forgotten. Too much, too
soon, too real,
No longer able to hide from it, or pretend it'll go
away.

Denial returns. Enjoying my final freedom. Time
stands still.

It began to get very foggy, quickly I was
forgetting more every day,
Confused, scared, grasping loved ones while I
still can,
Wasting no more time.

Memory's completely fading.

Reality and fantasy merge and become one in
my life.

Blissfully unaware.

Unknowingly scared.

Acceptance.

No concept of time.

What happened to me?
It all changed so quickly I was unable to see.
What happened when it all finally slowed down?
I was too far progressed in my Dementia,
I wouldn't know any different,
I now have a delusional and twisted perception
of reality in my mind.

Tell Me Again

Chapter 1: Can You Hear Me? - A Dementia Patient's View

Tell me again,
Take a second to remember,
It could be for so many different reasons,
I have a brain-deteriorating illness,
I'm not able to process things in the same way you will.

For example,
I could have gotten distracted,
I may genuinely not have been listening,
I may not have fully heard you, I may have hearing issues as well.
I may be pretending to ignore you as I'm embarrassed; to say I can't understand.

Tell me again,

Calmly. Slowly. Patiently.

I know I can be difficult and hard,
But take a deep breath in,
Imagine the confusion and frustration in me.

I mean, I'm now having to use my eyes to hear,
As I find it harder now to fully utilise my ears,
Reading lips is the only way I can communicate
properly,
Scared to admit they're now shutting down on
me too.

Masking my symptoms as long as I can.

Act Normal. Use tactics. Convince yourself
you're fine.

Tell me again, I don't understand,
Speak slowly, speak clearly, enunciate if you
can.

Tell me again, I've already forgotten,
My mind is in overdrive, no longer working.

Tell me again, no matter how many times I've
asked you,
Repetition and routine are stimulating my mind.

Tell me again, please don't get angry,
If I knew or remembered I wouldn't keep
asking.

Tell me again, no matter how seemingly small or
unimportant,

Include me, reassure me, be the peace my mind
never uncovers.

Tell me again,
I don't need to over-explain it.
Tell me again,
Tell me again.

I'm Scared!

Chapter 1: Can You Hear Me? - A Dementia Patient's View

When I cry and scream because I don't want to
get up,
Overreacting, physically trying to resist, or
causing pain and hurt,
Comfort and reassure me, I am terrified of
falling,
Help me, I need you, I'm scared!

A simple trip and fall for anyone in good health,
Will at most leave a bruise, a small mark, or sore
leg.
Me however, old in age, poor health, no mobility
left or stealth,
Will cause permanent deterioration and damage,
That's why I'm so scared of falling.

When I've had a fall, I become even more
anxious,
Unwilling to stand, or move, a statue stuck
sitting every chance I get to.
Nights alone, dark thoughts, scary dreams,
I don't want to be alone,
Help me, I'm so lonely and scared.

There are many things, old and newly
discovered, I fear,
If you listen and observe me closely enough,
My face, body, and mood will reflect when I
need protection.

If only you knew how many times a day I was in
genuine panic,
I look for you, I shout for you,
I need you,
I'm scared!

Just Say YES

Chapter 1: Can You Hear Me? - A Dementia Patient's View

Let's just be completely human and real,
Try your best to put yourself in my shoes,
If you had Dementia slowly deteriorating all that you are,
Wouldn't you just wish to do whatever you wanted,
Being your truest self, being who you really are?

Just say yes, allow me to live the end of my life to my very best!

If you were always weak, in pain, and half asleep,
Would you not want to be lazy? Lie in bed and rest finally,
After working and raising children for most of your earthly living years.

If I want to finally do nothing, literally stop and enjoy solitude and peace.
Who are you to question it, tell me otherwise, or disagree?
If I want to try new things, do things differently,

Welcome new opportunities and experiences to
me.

Just say yes, just say yes, just say yes, just say
yes!

If you started struggling to move, function and
walk,
Sore, scared and tired each time you simply
stood up.
If losing your mobility became inevitable,
Would you be scared, would you give up, would
you give it a good shot?

When all that can possibly be physically done,
has been tried and tested,
Is no longer effective or doing its job.
When I'm physically and mentally drained,
empty and broken,
Look out for me and give me what I want, what
I don't and what I need!

You always make sure my body's as clean as my
mind,
You grant my desires, dreams, and wishes,
Literally responsible for my whole existence
now in life.
Just say yes, just say yes, just say yes,

You know these sad eyes, and disappointed
facial expressions,
Pierce straight through to your heart, forever
close to your chest

I make no excuses, I justify myself no more, I no
longer take "no" for an answer,
Just say yes, just say yes, just say yes!

Through my eyes

I may be unknown, unspoken of in the stories
that you've thrown,
Defensively masquerading that I ever did exist,
Masking your own failures, maintaining the
façade you've always shown.
Pretending that you didn't dig the deadly pit of
your own abyss.
But still, I hold my head up high, and I just wish
you well.

Does my careless peace make you upset?
Why do you get mad when my name's
mentioned in a room?
Is it because I walk with such pride and
confidence?
Or is what does it, my heart of genuine gold?

As sure as time and the passing of the seasons,
With certainty that the sun will rise no matter the
reasons,
I'm awake, alive, as high as the sky, under a
euphoric spell,
But still, I just wish you well and peace of mind.

Did you enjoy crushing and breaking me down?
Fear-filled eyes, sealed lips, head to the ground.

Shuddering body, breath deepening, heart so
tight.
Did you notice all the fear, soulful screams and
tears?

Does my newfound empowerment offend you?
Do you sulk, obsess and take it harder each
time?
I can't help that I've uncovered my abundance,
Feel free to live regretfully, condemned,
following my life.

You can attack me with your words,
You can kill me in your mind,
You will however, never, live up to my magnetic
glowing light.
Still my dear, I wish you well in your life.
Does my radiant, dazzling beauty offend you
and fill you with rage?
Does it shine even brighter, more authentic, now
I'm away?
Does my rarity reflect, like a diamond in the
light?
It's clear what you've lost, I wish you well, I
wish you delight.

Burrowed up from the bottom of the deepest
darkest pit,

Emerging out of the shadows like a star on a
cloudy night,
Soaring up to the clouds, afar from a past
covered in pain and self-doubt,
Grounding myself, healing myself from a
lifetime of fight.

I am a free spirit, a powerful reckless force, a
forceful wind,
Letting nothing get in my way or what I want go
away in a whim,
Following my path breaking every barrier and
destructive facade,
No longer a victim, I let it all go, I hold the
power my ultimate force.

Allowing myself to be free of the agonising
trauma,
I wish myself well,
I wish myself a calm mind and wait for karma.

Blooming into my purest form, new calm aura
has finally begun,
I wish myself well,
I wish myself to believe in divine timing,
without even knowing it I've already
won.

Using the gifts that my life has given,

I wish myself well,
I wish myself blessings and blissful living.

I am the inspiration, the embodiment of faith,
I am the one who lives with gratitude,
I am the one that no matter what can't be pushed
down forever,
I am the survivor, the warrior, the powerful
magical woman.

I wish myself love, happiness and grace,
I wish to practice gratitude, honest living and
kindness always,
I wish to become the woman, who uses her
lessons to teach,

I wish to become an advisor, advocate and
supporter of sharing love and how
to heal.

But most of all, I wish myself well,
I wish myself well physically, emotionally and
spiritually blessed.
I wish myself well, I wish it for everyone, we all
deserve our minds at rest.

Do I Know What Dementia Is?

Deafening silence, as my brain starts to forget.
Echoes of all your voices, as my mind slowly
drifts away.
Melancholy music on repeat in my head.
Endless everlasting changes, as I become
blissfully unaware.
Nauseating nostalgia, angry as I no longer
remember "those days".
Timeless transitions overcoming my whole
being.
Impossible possibilities, as my body deteriorates
loudly.
Assuring acquiesce, I surrender, no choice but to
accept.

The Lost Maze

In the very early stages,
I struggled to carry out my daily duties,
Disorientated judgment,
Small problems grew larger than life.

I struggled to make easy decisions,
I got mixed up and forgot things so fast,
I was unable to hold a conversation,
I was lost but still very much alive.

As the middle stages rapidly crept in,
Repetition, repetition, repetition,
Impulsive speech and behaviours,
Not recognising most people or things.

I deludedly changed my perceptions,
I "overreacted" to things only I see,
I can't use my voice and jumble up words,
I lose more memories each moving day.

Within my final stage,
"Sorry, once more what did you say?"
Non-verbal, no voice, unable to understand,
Distress, numb emotions, non-expression of my
thoughts, my hollow mind empty and astray.

I'm lost in time, picturing myself as a child,
I'm looking at myself boldly blissfully blind,
I'm unable to place you or remember your name,
I'm deteriorating daily, my mind, my soul, my
body.

What Does It Really Feel Like – A Dementia Patient's Firsthand Account

This poem was inspired by a work activity created by me for residents to partake in. I sampled and tested it for the purpose of writing this poem with one resident initially.

The resident was given a spider diagram with ten branches for words to be filled in as to what words the resident associates most with their Dementia journey.

Once the resident had chosen the top ten words, they would use to describe Dementia, I was challenged to write a poem from their perspective including each of the ten chosen words.

The ten words are listed below:

1. Quiet
2. Changes
3. Forgetful
4. Stressed
5. Embarrassed
6. Scared
7. Confused
8. Boredom
9. Angry
10. Lonely

I suppose I'll find, I lost myself before I even
knew,
The mind becomes dark, blank and lost,
Constant fog, numbness, forgetful hues,
Everything is quiet, silent, light and soft,

Am I trapped or protected from reality?
Ignorant or innocent to the pain and loss?
When did I become out of touch and unaware?
Where deep in my mind can I find myself and
have a cognitive rebirth?
What do I remember about my Dementia
journey mostly?

I remember feeling weird, alone, in denial and
confused,
Everything changes in an instant, intensely,
swiftly and with force,
Emotionally overwhelmed, burnt out, exhausted,
overused,
Absently presents distantly far my presence,
masking the agony within.

Is it really a blessing disguised as a curse?
Or is my delusion and clouded vision deadly?
Is the curse that I'm paranoid and weak?
Or is my lack of awareness simply gentle and
free?

I feel angry all the time, irritated, resentful and
overwhelmed,
I feel embarrassed and ashamed, my ego
shattered, unable to be repaired,
I feel misunderstood, misinterpreted and
misrepresented.

Does it ever get better, if not, will I just seize the
day instead?
Do I remember who I really am?
Can I just decide, will I give up, or will I try?

I suffer in many ways, I'm so chill, yet so
stressed,
My boredom however, that's the real killer,
I've lost my passions, my comforts, my
livelihood, my old friends.

I wonder, does anyone else feel the same?
Do you feel so delusional, empty, surviving,
wise, old and sane?

I fear I'll be lonely, forgotten, faced to live the
end alone.
I'm scared of all that has happened, but mostly
I'm scared to be unalive.
I guess all the significant information, has just
been written for itself.

What do I associate with my Dementia journey?

I guess, a whirlwind of overwhelming emotions,
My physical health rapidly breaking and
shutting down,
Short intense moments shortly forgotten,
A time for reminiscing, and once unable to feel
loved and safe.

I suppose, we'll find, I am a new me, the one
you all know well,
My mind may be broken, but love gives me joy
and light,
A single star in the night sky shining,
Everything may not be good, but you can make
me feel warm again.

Acceptance

Tick…
      Tick…
            Eerie silence…

whisper

My brain goes tinggg…
                Head in a rattle…

Cling! Clang!
        C
          L
            A
              T
                T
                  E
                    Rrrrrr…

There's nothing I can do now but make each
minute count,
The worse my condition has gotten, the more I
just want to live free and light,
This is my home now, I need to embrace it.

I accept what my life is,
I accept nothing can change it,

I'm exactly where I need to be now
I choose peace, safety, and love.

My life is very empty and fearful,
My mind is fuzzy, blurry, and hazed,
My body shuts down, aches, and breaks,
Leaves me tearful, in pain, and stuck.

The brain fogs and numbly stops,
But in this acceptance, I find solace,
In the quiet chaos of my mind,
I discover a new kind of peace,
A gentle surrender to the unknown,
In this acceptance, I find my home.

What Can We Do?

There's nothing I can do now,
I try not to think about it,
No matter what I do now,

My mind is cloudy,
My body in overdrive.
I try to just ignore it,
I know I have Dementia,
We don't need to discuss it,
Just do something I like with me,
Make me smile for a day.

A Fresh Start

I used to fear becoming all I stood against,
The opposite of my true self,
One with cheeky comments and disrespect.

Rather I was given, a blank canvas,
A chance to start new and fresh,
A new thrilling chapter to my story.

I have become the woman I feared I'd become most,
A relentlessly honest open-mouthed serpent,
Not a care in the world, just saying whatever I want.

My mind's in a bubble,
My mouth's on a frenzy,
My attitude is terrible,
My body's ready to fight you, need I have to kick off.

Deadly Alive

My mind feels as though it's on another planet,
I'm half way into reality and halfway into my
envisions.

My body, yet so lively, floods buckets of pain,
It's falling apart in-front of me, yet half of me
doesn't even care.

My soul has been lost for a very long time,
I've lost my life goals, my real purpose in life.

My emotions are numb, blinded by my own
whirlwind of a mind,
My feelings turned off, all real meaning has
been lost.

I'm alive but I'm not really living,
I'm in touch with reality,
I'm also however deep in my own world,
I'm surviving but I'm not really living.

My personality becomes hostile and unkind,
I no longer control it, my body reacts and
subconsciously decides.

My behaviour becomes unpredictable and totally
out of character,
Aggression, repetition, delirium, oblivious
outbursts out of control.

Losing interest in my interests and passions,
Abandoning my daily routines, hobbies and
personal habits.

My whole persona I built my full life, irrelevant,
Carefully composed details chaotically
exploding recklessly without any
thought.

I'm alive but I'm not really living,
I'm myself but someone very different,
I'm similar but different,
I'm battling mental and physical prison.

It is what it is

There's nothing we can do now,
It's beyond unnecessary repair time.

My life is one big impossible puzzle,
You'll never understand it till you have it.

I don't wanna waste time talking about it,
It is what it is now, peace only in my life.

Self Realisation

Even on my very worst days,
I'm forced to pick myself up,
Get washed, dressed, eat and socialise,
Although not always appealing,
It fills my days with purposeful worth.

Free

In the realm of last lights straying,
Memories muddled, mixed and fraying.
Mind mazed into futile fragments,
Thoughts wild in whimsical whispering
windfalls.

Familiar faces heedlessly hazing,
Names needless to say forgotten in faith failed.

Disarrayed maze.

Time entangles, days duplicate, memory
mangled,
Paradoxical past, present and prospects,
Indefinitely undefined.

Momentarily I remember,
My whole Identity remains no more,
So differently unknown…

Am I lost, newfound or losing my mind???
I listen to the voices,
Yet they're thunderously tranquil.

Amidst all anarchy,

Flickers of fantasy. Faithful fighting. Future
flight.

The mind might "boggle",
My spirits however forever in morrow,
Newborn freedom is blissful bewilderment.

For the sake of God and all the good I have lived
for,

My wings are wilfully wide open…

Finally,
         I AM
                F
                 R
                  E
                   E
                    E
                       EEEEEEE.

To finish Grant me one last wish

If I can grant a request from thee,
Remember me as I wanted,
Use my memory wisely,
To learn or inspiration for creativity.

Don't waste time with sadness,
Smile for me, I'm finally free,
Take my hand, it's always there to hold,
I've elevated up, found peace in solace.

If you feel a void or alone,
Please fill it with my presence,
Remember me joyously,
Miss me, but use it as fuel to do more.

Each time it hits you, follow the moon or sun,
They promise to rise each morning,
And fall out of site, into darkness evermore,
Find the light, the glimmer, the shine.

Perhaps it's hard for you to grasp,
My time was quick, hard, brief,
Don't waste more time with heartache and grief,

Use your heart, soul and mind, embody yourself
in me.

My Meticulous Memory

In my memory,
I'd like it to be positive,
I'd like to heal and inspire,
Leave an everlasting imprint,
Of self-love and discovery.

I'd like to leave waves of motion,
Whispers of softness, power and empathy,
Times of happiness, full of laughter and joy,
A spark, flame, or light, in thought, I'm spirit, or
in person.

I'd like the sad thoughts,
The tears of grief and sorrow,
To dry with fire fuelled from passion,
To dry under the sunlight,
To be used only as inspiration towards goals.

To you I have died over and over,
To myself I've been reborn several times,
To us all I'm still here in spirit,
But gone is my persona, my soul and my mind,
The stress and changes aren't of real importance.

For yes I have been diagnosed with Dementia,
I get confused easily and fail to understand,

My body is still full of drive, determination not
to give in,
My mind however has drifted much further,
inevitably begun to uncontrollably
crumble.

So you've already made your peace,
Maybe even said your final goodbyes,
But here we celebrate someone new,
For it's not how they act, or how they're
perceived,
It's the connection, love and bond you share that
keeps you together
spiritually.

My Memorial

And so, here we finally have it,
Time to remember, reflect and to share,
Did my wishes manifest in to focus,
What final imprint do you all hold to clear,
In my memory, what am I?

When you're toasting the end of my living,
Do you remember my true, honest,
Faithful, helpful vision,
For I was true to myself until the very end,
Me, myself and I reliving over and over.

We recognise you as your best self,
We speak of your younger, livelier days,
We concentrate on the good times,
We try to remember you the way you wanted,
We realise that your life was much longer than
your disease.

If you look at the bigger picture,
We still had many more lovely healthy years,
The illness was much shorter,
Than the impact and inspiration that you shared,
Your life was so long and beautiful, we speak of
it each and every day.

We think of you as the pictures in our albums,
We think of when you were fit and full of beans,
We think of you in all of your glory,
When asked by others about you,
It's only these things that we tell.

And so we meet in mind and memory,
Memory of a mind that once was,
One so tender, deep and devoted to cause,
Here to pay final tributes and respects,
One final goodbye and love you.

A Letter to You: Dear Un-dearest Dementia – From A Dementia Survivor

Dear Un-Dearest Dementia,

I write to you blissfully blind and relentlessly resilient, no longer allowing you to define my existence. I want to express my gratitude for the lessons you have taught me, even though they took time and togetherness away. You have challenged me in ways I never thought possible, but I refuse to let you define me. Thank you for giving me on final chance to go out fighting full of pride, full of face, full of faith!

Let me be clear, when it comes to what you bring, I stand by only one thing and that is showing your subtly severe secrets of universally unspoken upset, unknown answers and Dementia caused damage and pain. Despite your attempts to break me down, I have found solace in the support and love of those around me.

We all have, one common goal, one common
good, one coming outcome!
We will continue to conquer self-doubting
powers and limitations,
We will continue to find new powers of spirit
and silence,
We will continue to disallow you to consume
and control,
We will continue to find purpose and defy odds
living more each day.

You may have invaded my life, unable to
typically define me,
What more can you do? I fight against your
forceful grip,
I'm rising up, surpassing expectations for
victory,
You've taken so much from me but my will to
live remains strong,
I will never back away, or let you take me lying
down.

Dementia, I acknowledge your presence, but
from this moment forward, I release any
negative thoughts or attachments towards you. I
will no longer waste any words, time or attention
towards your nonexistence. I am reclaiming my
life and wish for your ceaseless demise. May
you fade away into oblivion.

Please consider this as official documentation
terminating my relationship with you. If you
have any questions, confusion, or require any
further clarification. Shove it where the sun
don't shine and please do not ever reach out
again.

I wish you nothing but death,
I wish you nothing but to become extinct,
I wish you the worst luck in your future
endeavours,
I wish you no thanks or success.

Respectfully, I decline to acknowledge you any
further,

With unwavering determination,

A survivor who refuses to be defined by you and
your existence.

Chapter 2: Can You Still See Me? - A Dementia Survivor's Loved One's View

Poem No.

To My Mum

Chapter 2: Can You Still See Me? - A Dementia Survivor's Loved One's View

As deep as I am, I swallow my pride,
Hiding my agonising cycle of grief,
Broken and empty inside.
Pain weakly hidden within fake hope and smiles,
A boy, teen, or man will always need a mum in
their life.

I think deeply about our time together, you've
been my rock,
My inspiration through each stage of my life.

I prematurely reminisce, I regret, feel guilt for
all of my mistakes,
Wishing I'd given you the world served on a
golden plate.

I know you are proud, and will always be my
biggest supporter and guide,
You taught me how to be a parent, be
independent and build a stable life.

Although I'll always know how much you loved
us all,

I wonder, and wish still, that I could hear your
current thoughts.

I'm thanking and blaming you for teaching me
traditional old ways,
I've created my own version, the perfect old and
modern balance.
Due to old-time stigmas, as a man, I struggle to
talk or share.
I close up. Stay silent. Unspoken words. Get on
with it. Push it all away.

You made me who I am, a real man and
respectable gent,
Shaped my mind and drive, to get me a better
life than the one you bared.

Little do you know I've done it all to impress
you, each detail of me you in every way,
I only ever wanted to make you proud and put a
smile on your face.

I only cry in secret, as not to phase you or upset
you, I face uncontrollable anger and feel so
confused,
Devastated Dementia decided it would be you,
Why would it target an angel, why would they
take away you?

My beautifully sculpted mother, elegant,
timeless, and always been there,
Suffering endlessly and unjustly, and there's
nothing anyone can do to make it go away or
change.

I hold on to our memories, thankful for our
endless bond that can't be taken away.
A mother, a wife, family, worker, friend,
The rock of the family, the strong warrior.
So strong, courageous and brave.

I grieve over and over as you change constantly
and fade away,
I however focus on the positive times, the love
and beauty you radiate.

Praying, practicing gratitude, and taking
advantage of every new day,
Dreading the fateful day yet to come, where
you'll forever be taken away.

My Gran Has Dementia

Chapter 2: Can You Still See Me? - A Dementia
Survivor's Loved One's View

I don't fully remember the first time I found out,
I just remember it being hard and being sad
every day, every little while.
When I realised Dementia had captured my
gran, my thoughts and emotions were spinning
around.

I remember some things clearly, things that have
just clearly stuck with me.

Seeing my dad cry for the first time,
Wailing on his knees.
Seeing my Grampa get extremely depressed,
and become limp, lifeless, and lose all hope in
humanity.

I have experienced a lot of darkness, sadness,
and traumatic scenes,
The whole family dynamic disintegrating in
front of me.

The gran I always knew, drifting further and
further away,

No longer able to picture her, I forget how she
used to look.
I forget what she used to be like, generally, with
myself, at any other time.
I forget how she used to act, how she spoke, how
she used certain words.
I forget how she moved, how she danced, or
even walked around.

My gran has Dementia, that much I know!
I'll shout it loud and proudly, for all to hear and
support.
My gran has Dementia, let's stop the
awkwardness, silence, and fear to say it out loud.
It isn't taboo, insensitive, or unkind, to mention
the word "Dementia",
Rather the opposite, educational, considerate,
and necessary to get the word out.

I reminisce and often think back, as she always
had a bad memory, and mixed things up,
Calling us all the wrong names, mixing up
birthdays, forgetting the oven's been on for over
an hour to bake cupcakes.
She always made us laugh with her daily
forgetful mishaps,
It's who she's always been, at least that's never
changed.

We laugh now when we think of the irony, that
the most forgetful woman born,
Ended up with Dementia, as we always joked,
she was born with it imbedded into her brain.
That's why it took so long to accept it, and get it
diagnosed,
Over five years we suspected and got her tested
for it,
Told over and over, "unconfirmed", "conflict of
opinions" and straight" no's".

She suffered the illness much longer than it took
us to discover it,
Which is a blessing and a curse,

If we knew sooner, we could've gotten help
quicker, asked for more of her opinions on how
she'd like her life to be handled when it's on her
behalf,
When she's no longer able to think for herself
and consciously choose.
We could've had more time to plan, and give her
better opportunities.

However, it may also be good we were blind to
time, as we spent sentimental time together,
No worries, no stress, five full years of carefree
memories,

and unknowingly granting your wishes and last
requests.

I find it quite full circle that our elders teach us
how to love and care,
If honoured with the privilege we can give them
it all back,
I guess the silver lining is that I cherish our time
more, than I ever did before,
That I'm able to selflessly take care of you and
be trusted so visibly deep.

My gran has Dementia, she's not the woman she
used to be.

My gran has Dementia, you need to now love
and treat her more delicately.

From Wife To Worn Out

Chapter 2: Can You Still See Me? - A Dementia
Survivors Loved Ones View

When did it change?
When did my wife become a stranger I had to
relearn?

How did I not see it?
The woman I love most captured by the horrible
disease.

Where is her mind?
Why's it so different?

How does she view me?
I wonder if she still adores me.

Am I still her forever, her voice one and only?
Does she know how much I admire every part of
her being?

I noticed her drifting, distant and estranged,
Memories, thoughts, and words fading,
Refusing to believe this is our fate.

I laugh when I remember, you kicking me out of
the bed,

In each hand we hold the ash that smokes
through each room, forcing a blaze from a single
match.

I feel helpless when I think of how social you
once were,
To you now being stuck in, limited, and missing
out.

We planned our retirement together,
Never imagining it would begin and end like
this,
But I would never change it as I will always love
and care for you as long as we both live.

Different dreams. Change of routine. Adapting
to a new way of living.

It did all change, but it's not all bad, is it?
My wife's still the most important thing to me.

I see it all clear now,
Helping my remarkable wife fight daily.

I know it may all be different now, but some
things remain the same.

My wife may be worn out now,
But she always has protection in me.

Unrecognisable

Chapter 2: Can You Still See Me? - A Dementia
Survivor's Loved One's View

I look at them in the eyes,
With disgust they turn away,
Such deep loving blue eyes,
Saying "Please get away from me."

Why do they scowl and turn away from me?

Is it them?

Is it me?

Is it disgust they really do see?

I wonder how they think now, and what they
must feel,
Do they still love me?
Do they feel trusted and safe with me?

I can't tell what they're thinking,
No emotions, words, or actions.
Having to build a brand new relationship,
Starting to learn the new them super fast.
I look at them in admiration, and smile subtly,

Their head slowly turns, locking eyes piercingly
with me,
They smile with pure glee and mouths "love" for
all to see.

They quickly lose interest and stop
acknowledging me.

I wonder and question if they really recognise
me,
Know how much they love me, equally knowing
I share the same depth of love,
And feel connected spiritually to me as we are
soul family.

They don't show me any attention as long as I'm
there,
But show me the love and connection will
always be there.
Upon leaving, they sit up beaming with pride,
cuddling me goodbye, saying 'I love you'
although no words come out.

They may be completely unrecognisable,
But they remain so predictably recognisable.

The One I Ache For

Chapter 2: Can You Still See Me? - A Dementia
Survivor's Loved One's View

It kills me inside and breaks my heart,
When I see you hurt this way.

The pain of watching you suffer,
That helpless feeling of uselessness.

You are my family, even if you forget,
I ache in pain watching you in distress.
You are my family, I'll never let you forget!

I struggle to adapt, accept the change will last.

Conforming to a new version of your former
self,
Reintroducing the new you,
Meeting ourselves again for the first time.

I found it challenging at first to communicate
with you,
But now I find it harder just not being there with
you.

I find it hard to watch you suffer,

Unable to take it all away,
But I find it even harder to watch you transform
in such a negative way.

I'm still finding my way to show you I love you,
I find it easy to discover new ways to do so, as
your essence is powerful and inspires.

I get emotional when I think of the past,
I get thankful for the time we still share and
have,
But mostly I prepare for the final day, as I can
never imagine my life without you in it and
there.

It kills me, my heart aches when I think of you
that way,
Seeing my life without you makes it seem too
much to bear.

To the one I ache for, you'll never ache alone.

Grief, Grief, Grief

Chapter 2: Can You Still See Me? - A Dementia Survivor's Loved One's View

The cycle of grief goes back and forth, you lose your loved ones over and over,
Through each change in their physical state or mental,
And through every deterioration.

The initial shock from finding out, embedded with denial and prayers of doubt.

Shortly after the pain starts to kick in, both physical and mental, the mind begins to change.

Guilt and regret start to sink in,
Missed opportunities seem like the most important thing.

Lashing out, shouting, being angry, aggressive, and full of rage.

Confusion, shock and fear overrule my emotions and make me feel despair.

Sadness, depression, no motivation,

Giving up hope,
Nothing seems worth it.

Suddenly, acceptance and understanding start to
kick in.

Grief, grief, grief,

It comes and goes in waves,
Stages interchanging,
Something that always stays,
And never goes away.

Can You Still See Me? - Is this our last "I love you"

Chapter 2: Can You Still See Me? - A Dementia Survivor's Loved One's View

Can you still see me?

Can you still hear my voice?

Will this time be our final goodbye?

Is today's "I love you" going to be the last?

Can you still feel me?

Can you still memorise me when I'm away?

I feel overseen yet still misunderstood.

Can you please just give me a sign?

Do I know what dementia is?

A shadowed mind, a fading bliss.
Lost in memories, a tangled maze,
A loved one's light begins to haze.

In their eyes, a distant stare,
A soul adrift, unaware.
Fragments of the past, now gone,
Leaving us to carry on.

Do I know what dementia is?
A cruel thief, a silent abyss.
But still, in moments fleeting,
Love remains, forever beating.

Let me In

Let me in, let me in, they softly plea,
To the heart that once knew them so well.
Through the fog and the haze, they strain to see,
The memories, the love, the stories they tell.

Their eyes may not recall, their words may stray,
But deep within, their spirit still shines bright.
A flicker of recognition, a fleeting ray,
A connection that transcends the fading light.

So hold their hand, embrace them tight,
For in that moment, they are here with you.
Let love be the guiding star in the night,
And cherish the bond that forever holds true.

Let me in, let me in, they whisper soft,
To the soul that still beats strong and clear.
In the dance of life, no matter how aloft,
Love is the melody they long to hear.

How could I compare?

How could I compare, to a fading star,
A loved one slipping, lost and far?
Like a puzzle missing its key,
Dementia steals what used to be.

Memories scattered, like leaves in the wind,
A once sharp mind now worn and thinned.
How can I hold on to what once was,
As time erases, with its relentless pause?

How could I compare, to a fading light,
A shadowed presence, out of sight?
But in my heart,

How to carry a caseload

In the shadows of dementia's grip,
I bear a burden that's hard to ship.
A caseload heavy with care and love,
Guiding them through the mists above.

Each day a journey, fraught with fears,
Navigating through their shifting gears.
A load I carry with tender hands,
Supporting them through life's shifting sands.

In their world of confusion and haze,
I walk beside them, through the maze.
Shouldering their struggles, big and small,
For in their eyes, I see it all.

So I carry this caseload, heavy and true,
With patience, compassion, and love anew.
For in their hearts, my presence stays,
A guiding light through the foggy days.

My final words

In the twilight of my days,
I gather my thoughts in a haze.
Reflecting on a life well-lived,
And all the love that I have given.

My final words, a whispered prayer,
For those I leave behind to bear.
May you find solace in memories sweet,
And in the love that will never deplete.

Let not sorrow cloud your days,
But bask in the sun's warm rays.
For I'll be watching from above,
Surrounded by eternal love.

So cherish the moments we shared,
For in your hearts, I'll always be there.
My final words, a gentle goodbye,
As I spread my wings and take to the sky.

Sacred

In the quiet of the sacred night,
Where stars above shine pure and bright.
I feel a presence, calm and serene,
A divine energy, yet unseen.

In the whispers of the gentle breeze,
I sense a sacred, ancient ease.
A connection to the earth and sky,
A bond that will never die.

In the silence of the sacred space,
I find peace, a holy grace.
A sanctuary for my soul to rest,
In the sacredness I am blessed.

Tongue-tied

In the shadows I carry long when you're gone,
A light flickers at the end, faintly
In the shadows of dementia's grasp,
A loved one's light begins to lapse.

Memories fading, slipping away,
Leaving hearts heavy, in disarray.
Their once-vibrant spirit, now adrift,
Lost in a fog, a memory rift.

We hold onto moments, fleeting and dear,
Trying to keep their essence near.
In the silence of their vacant stare,
We see the person who once was there.

A bittersweet ache, a constant pain,
Watching them slip away, in vain.
But in the depths of this challenging plight,
"Oh so slick and sly.

In a world of clichés, where phrases roam,
Words tongue-tied, in a linguistic dome.
Playing with well-known sayings, oh so sly,
Twisting and turning, with a clever eye.

Like a needle in a haystack, hard to find,
Or a diamond in the rough, one of a kind.
We're walking on eggshells, oh so delicate,
While chasing rainbows, forever intricate.

The early bird catches the worm, they say,
But the cat's got your tongue, come what may.
A penny for your thoughts, a drop in the bucket,
With a chip on your shoulder, just pluck it.

So let's paint the town red, with flying colors,
And turn over a new leaf, like no others.
In this game of clichés, we're tongue-tied,
But the show must go on, with pride.

Speak to Me

There must be a way,
What else can I learn,
What's on your mind?
How can I make you open up?
How can I get you to trust me once more?
What do you see?
What do you need?
What do you feel?
There must be something,
What else is there to do?
What is your body telling me?
How can you tell me in your own way?
How can you trust the unknown even once?

If there's one thing I wanted it was,
For you to let me in!
Now I realise it's down to me,
As long as I'm there,
Our bond will always be imbedded deep,
I let myself, let you in!

Fate

As I lay butt bare,
Surrendering my scars of war,
I give you all my monstrous mess,
Thickly black coated ashes,
Deeply pitted into each word.

As I stone my sword,
Conceding to lifeless disarray,
I offer you my mud-coated memories,
Rooted deep in entanglement,
Ripped and shredded pages of ink stains.

As I bow my head,
Reminiscing my removed crown,
I leave you all my twisting turmoils,
Blackened canvases of colourful clandestine,
Smeared shadows of showering sunshine.

As I lay down my aching ardent arms,
Waving wistful white flags of whispers,
I impart my innermost introspective intel,
Trailing through tainted tracks,
of tarnished transformational traumatic triumph.

I embrace the badges of battlefield bruising,
The echoes of my past whispered through winds
of vines,
I entrust you with a symphony of scars, sabotage
and suffering in stories,
Resonating universal emotions, feelings,
strength and struggles,
For in my flawed farewell lies temples of
treasure.

Chapter 3: Can You Be Fully Represented Through Me? - A Dementia Carer/Support Worker's View

I Am What They Need Me To Be

Chapter 3: Can You Be Fully Represented Through Me? - A Dementia Carer/Support Worker's View

I am what they need me to be.

Nothing more, nothing less,

Just endless I profess,

I am what they need me to be!

"Treat them like family, but don't get too attached"

Chapter 3: Can You Be Fully Represented Through Me? - A Dementia Carer/Support Worker's View

The ones we care for, and spend time with the most,
Become the people closest to us,
Like family you love unconditionally,
Helping them heal and grow.

We are told to treat them like family,
But not get too attached,
It's impossible not to build personal bonds,
You are specially connected together for the journey, start to end.

How can I not get upset?
How can I not take it to heart?

For they're the ones we get to know best,
The ones we care for, learn inside out.
The ones we share most of our days with.

It's human nature to become like family,

It's human nature to get attached.
It's inevitable that relationships will bloom.

The bond between a carer and a patient is unique
and can never be matched.

I Know You Better Than I Know Myself

Chapter 3: Can You Be Fully Represented Through Me? - A Dementia Carer/Support Worker's View

It's ironic how a carer has better insight into their patients than their own self-identity and thoughts.
Spending each of our working days, living by their sides, learning all their loves and hates and what gives them meaning in life.
It's ironic how a carer, is a representative for all that the patient is, how they walk, talk, and live out each day.
Yet inside we struggle to care or look after ourselves.

How can it be that I know a stranger better than I'll ever know me,
A stranger that becomes one of the people we hold dearest and nearest, a big part of who I am, and shaping me,
Putting their worlds before our own, letting them live vicariously through my stories and watching them grow.

I find it strange how it comes to be, from a job to
a lifestyle, to your whole entirety.
I find it strange how I know what they'll say,
what they're thinking inside, how they are by
one look that day.
I find it strange how my whole world revolves
around the ones that I care for, not a second they
don't cross my mind.

Isn't it ironic how a carer knows you best, is
able to advocate for you, be your confidant and
friend.
The one who will fight for you until the very
end, and fight every day to make sure you're
heard and your needs are met.
It's ironic however a carer, cares so little about
themselves, yet uses their whole heart to care for
you in every way.
Repeated heartbreak, trauma, and hard work that
becomes,
Yet never second-guessed, or in question, as our
work is never done.

How can it be I know you better than my own,
my loved ones, my friends, my colleagues and
more,
A resident, a patient, are offensive words to me,
as you're individually all equally special to me,

Forever I'll love you, and do right by you when I
can, obsessed with your presence,
A relationship so unique, no one will fully
understand.

I find it strange how you become my family,
everything I could aspire, and aim to ever be.
I find it strange how I don't have to ask, how
you feel, what you wish, or when you just need a
heart or a hand.
I find it strange that no matter how difficult, I
wouldn't change it, a lifelong bond built, forever
sacred, broken never.

It's ironic how bittersweet it is to be a carer,
moments full of joy and love suffocated with
agonising loss and pain.
Spending each minute by each other's side,
learning how to love and lose you in such a short
period of time.
It's ironic how something so rewarding can also
be so disappointing, investing yourself in a
person, just to have them ripped away.
Yet still we continue to love and care, knowing
they matter more than ourselves.

I know you better than I know myself, I count
myself grateful to get to know you that well.
I know you better than I know myself.

I Cry, I Grieve, I'm Traumatised!

Chapter 3: Can You Be Fully Represented Through Me? - A Dementia Carer/Support Worker's View

My job is full of ups and downs, twists and turns, wrongs and rights,
It's one of the most challenging careers, with plenty of rewards if you can hold off long enough for them to appear.

The bonds you make can never be undone, a newfound family, chosen through passion and exceptional love.
The job itself is so very small, it's the people you meet that matter, and their stories that live on.

It's never any easier to see them deteriorate or decline, to watch them as they slowly pass away into the clouds.
I think I'll always suffer, and struggle to accept, that all these gentle wholesome souls don't have much time left.

I cry, I grieve, I'm traumatised!
Each time I face a new goodbye.

My job is full of heartbreak, predicting loss and
pain,
Yet each time I lose someone it feels the same,
the grief never goes away.

The strength of character it takes to remain, to
continue in your role, sharing overbearing
positivity whilst feeling utter shame,
The strength it takes in your mind and your body
is something you gain through multiple
hauntings.

It causes many phases, being numb, being lost,
being broken,
Or builds up your resilience, making you
compassionate and over-caring.
Sometimes it makes you, other days it breaks
you, yet your emotions always neutrally in
place.

I cry, I grieve, I'm traumatised!
Each time I say hello to a new face.

Its cheerful melancholy, a sheer oxymoron in
itself,
To love, to hold, to cherish,

Then to watch it all helplessly while it's ripped
completely away.

I hold such pride and honour that I'm able to
play such a vital role,
Eternally thankful and grateful for being able to
offer you all I have and more.

I think of all we've shared, how I never expected
such a change,
The sweetest, kindest person, in total disarray.
I struggle as I watch you slowly become
someone else, a totally alternate person, in the
same body I've always held.

I cry, I grieve, I'm traumatised!
Each time the cycle's reborn.

I cry, I grieve, I'm traumatised!
I hide it all behind closed doors.

I cry, I grieve, I'm traumatised!
I pretend to be okay.

I cry, I grieve, I'm traumatised!
I'm only human at the end of the day.

UNDER and OVER

Under vs Over:

Underpaid for all that we do,
Overworked and expected to do it.

It's nobody's fault,
It's just the way it is.

The health and social care sector is
under-resourced and underfunded,

Overwhelming workloads, overloaded with
responsibilities,
Over stigmatised negative portrayals, tarring all
of us untrustworthy, lazy, and uneducated.

Overburdened and underestimated,
Assumptions and judgments form naturally.

Overstimulated, with over expectations,
Undervalued and appreciated we remain.

It's Harder Than It Seems: Tears, Stress, Triggers and Struggles.

Chapter 3: Can You Be Fully Represented Through Me? - A Dementia Carer/Support Worker's View

There are so many rewarding aspects to being a carer, and it really is an honourable job to work in. I would like to clarify I love my job more than anything, and have always been passionate about helping others.

However, like everything in life, there are a lot of challenges. Mentally, physically, emotionally, and socially.

It's harder than it seems, spending most of your working life with those you care for,
You get attached like family, take your work worries and stress back home.

It's hard in many ways, some obvious, some overlooked.

On days there're lots of challenges,
Things going wrong,
It all becoming too much,
When you can feel yourself ready to explode.

It's harder than it looks to compose yourself, stay
professional, and bite your tongue.

Many tears have been shed,
A result of a bad day,
Being injured or hurt,
Losing one of our deeply loved residents,
Or being triggered from our personal hurt.

It's harder than it looks to hide your hurt and
hold your emotions back.

Endless stress, dealing with literal people's lives.
No matter how patient, empathetic, or kind,
We all have moments we feel anger and
frustration.

Stress felt for each resident whenever they're
distressed or in pain.
Stress felt for families and loved ones as we can
understand how lost they feel.
Stress felt for the home itself, as keeping up with
policies, procedures, and changing rules is
overwhelming.

Stress felt for ourselves trying to balance, juggle,
and manage residents, as well as our own
individual lives.

It's harder than it looks managing yourself
properly in a high stress and fast environment.

Constantly facing our own emotions, and taking
them on for everyone else.
Trying to recognise triggers for Dementia
patients,
Whilst overcoming personal triggers for
yourself.

It's harder than it looks taking on the stress and
worries of others, it's even harder when you
have your own personal stress and worries.

The struggles you face are incomparable and
endless,
They span from yourself, to loved ones and
friends, and especially the ones with Dementia
who suffer.

"S" is for strength of character that each carer
builds
"T" is for tears, triggers and trauma. Tenacity, in
which we grow through our difficult challenges

"R" is for respect, resilience and reflection. Remarkable acts of service delivered every day.

"U" is for understanding, unity and uniqueness. Unconditional love and kindness and advocating for patients.

"G" is for gratitude, grace and guidance. Giving it their all and looking on the bright side.

"G" is also for genuine love and care.

"L" is for love and life. Living in the moment and supporting changes that arise.

"E" is for empowerment, encouragement and effective. Excellence in all that you do.

It's harder than it looks, dealing with hard struggles.

It's harder than it looks, being a carer, and it revolving around your whole life.

Glue

If there was one word I could use to describe
how I felt,
It would be spell, under which, of yours I melt.
My spirit broken, worn and warm in solitude,
Overused and abused, completely self-refused.
Although despite of it all, with you I feel whole,
You are the glue to my bond,
Once stuck on my heart, never to become
undone.
Piece by piece we pick up torn-up words,
Whenever I see you, wherever that may be,
I realise we have each other.

You're stuck to me like glue,
We come together,
One whole from, two a piece.

Eyes of The Beholder

Who am I? That depends on who you ask…
I am the caregiver, the most intrusively close
person to you.
I am the watcher, the one who notices changes
and knows your facial tells.
I am the guide, the most crucial person to help
you understand and decide.
I am the smile amongst sorrow, the one who
gives you a warm embrace.
I am the compass to guide you to lands
unknown, the most important one to
remind you of home and your safe place.
I am the person who wants to give you it all, the
most caring person you'll find,
the one who will put you above all.

Silent Struggles

I shall do my best to do all you have asked,
I shall however blame myself when something
falls through or apart.
I shall do my best not to fail you,
I shall however shed tears or disappointment
when I can't fulfil your wish.
I shall do my best to love you in every way,
I shall however feel sadness over moments not
so pleasant, full of disarray.
I shall do my best to be your pillar of strength,
I shall however crumble as I leave, taking it
home with me.
I shall always give you endless love and care,
I shall however die inside each time you feel
down or not yourself each day.

Battles of The Brain

The brain bewilders as I think of you and me,
The endless empathetic compassionate
commotion,
The never-ending blessing and blows,
The battles of the brain.
The body fails to burn out as I lose sleep over
your mind, body and personality
changes,
The continuous circle of creation,
The leg shaking, lifeless, lucid dreaming,
The battles of the brain.
The voice projecting silence as I become a
nocturnal vigil,
Each breath, a painful swallow to intake,
The muted communication,
The battles of the brain.

A Shoulder To Lean On

I can be a hand for you to hold,
An arm you can reach out to,
A heart to hold onto and give it right back.
I can be a voice to advocate and acknowledge
you,
A head to think for you and keep memories alive
for both our sakes,
A leg to stand on when you feel unbalanced or
unsafe.
I can be a shoulder to lean on,
Lay your head down
Wrap your arms around,
I can be a person who will always protect you,
Who won't ever leave,
Who will forever be there and stay.

Embracing Emotions

I've faced my fears of intense inside intimately
intrusive thinking,
Embracing my emotions,
Finally choosing to feel all that you present to
me.

May your hands ever be stable,
May I be a helping one when you need support
for anything.

May your stomach always be stuffed and strong,
May I offer you feelings of safety, offering you
peace and a chance to break
down your tough towers so tall.

May your legs not grow weak or weary,
May I walk with you and lift you up when you
can no longer fathom the torturous travel and
concede or cave.

May your mind always be full and free,
May I give you useful knowledge and help you
to be peacefully pleased.

May your heart be blessed, fulfilled and open,

May I give you a safe place to confide in and
feel important.

Finally I allow myself to embrace excessive
emotions,
The good, bad or unexplained,
Emotionally I feel grateful, for all I get to
embody and express.

Shine

The thing I want the most is just to see you
shine.
I put aside the legalities, I just want you to be a
staple of inspiration,
You know moments like,
"Omg, when I'm that age, I hope that's what I
turn out like".
Whatever your life dreams and goals are,
I just want to see you shine in them,
Exceeding limitations of life.
In spite of all the seriousness,
I just want you to remember who you really are,
I want you to own your identity,
Take centre stage and shine like a newfound
light turning star.

Bountiful Bonds

In a book or discovery, where time moves faster
than a moment to think,
Stand so achingly still and absent,
Bountiful bonds built from brave interactions.

A comfort concocting as easy as a cat's presence,
settling into a home and
marking territorial treason,

We navigate the maze, a
Bountiful bonds built in understanding the
patient's mind and reasoning.

Through gentle purrs and soft whispers,
connections combine,
Bountiful bonds, where compassion is pure,
Built from becoming you, when I need to
empathise mindfully and emotionally,
Bonds become stronger each and every time.

Magic Touch

In a world where you wilt and wander away,
I as your caregiver walks each path with you
every time you stray,
As the saying goes, "You do a hard job, I take
my hat off to you",
I'll always provide the magic touch, I'll always
give you what you need and
know before you do.

My touch, like magic, takes you to your comfort
and safe zone,
I will always get rid of your burdens that
dementia has given you or stole,
In delicate moments, I'll provide a smile that
lights up the grey.

In a world where you feel lost and forgotten,
I will always find you and navigate you towards
recognition of your legacy,
In uncertain fates, I'll create a haven, a place
called home for you to stay.

Through all the tears and laughter, I stand strong
beside you,
Hands warm to hold, help, heighten or heal you,
A caregiver's touch, pure light and love.

In the realm of dementia, you will never feel
alone,
Moments made are a memoir of art.
With every gesture, every caring clutch,
A caregiver's touch, provides magic, lifting and
healing each one they touch.

Symbolic Symphony

A dementia caregiver's heart will pay the cost,
In the silent realm of memories, life and love
gained and lost,
Thoughts tuning into symbolic symphony,
Fragments of feelings following our reality.

With tender touch and eyes truly open in glee,
Carers seek to unlock the hidden key to give
survivors' minds peace,
Tuning their thoughts into symbolic symphony.
Weaving together fragments of ourselves to
create life-changing movements
for our loved cared for residents that become
family.

A caregiver's heart, conducts complete
consistent routine,
A caregiver provides a symbolic symphony,
playing on and on to give you joy
and happiness at every chance I can get for thee.

A caregiver brings the rise of day and light to
each morning,
A caregiver ensures each nightfall prayers are
provided of promised peace,
A symphony of significant harmony,

Symbolically sparking new limits and means of life.

Breath, break, begin again

As a caregiver I tread with love, spreading spirit,
Whilst up against the wall, challenged in every
possible being.

I remind myself…

Breathe,
      Break,
         Begin Again.

The cycle never ending,
Ever unfolding in-front of me,
In this journey of life, our story molds,
Through shattered pieces, together we learn to
repair.

With each new dawn, we embrace the past and
new possibilities and uncertainty causing
anxious overthinking overloaded.

I calmly refrain, I remind myself once again…

Breathe,
      Break,
         Begin Again.
Be the ease amidst the world of strain.

Journey Joined

It's true what they say, to share is to care,
In this journey joined and binder,
Our hearts woven in tapestry on the chest of our
inner minds.

A labyrinth treaded with careless intent,
An inevitable intertwined relationship,
Our deepest parts combined and outplayed.

Hand in hand, eye to eye, no words needed,
True raw emotions shared with just touch and
gaze.

In a chase to fulfil dreams in ticking time,
Souls dance in innocence,
Connect in companionship,
Hearts locked in and ready for all you need to
fill it right.

Coincidental Collisions

Coincidental calculated collisions,
Consciously lost, found and bound,
Chaotically combined, two strangers,
Cherishing each, lifelong bonds built bright.

Through years worth of connections,
I accept, each person serves a purpose in your
life,
Call it coincidence, control or chance,
Each connection formed, is destined to last.

In this coincidental collision, a story is created,
A carer's automatic universal pull,
A sacred mission for each person I reach,
Let's show devotion to our cause…

Let's honour whatever reason we were destined
to meet.

A distant dream

I wish I could gift you all of your dreams,
Although most remain distantly unreachable,
I wish I could take you out to smell the leaves
when it rains,
I wish I could gift you the noise of the park, the
crisping rustle of leaves,
I'll do my best to make reality out of a distant
dream.

Poem No.

1. Dementia for Dummies- A Guide of Common Sense
2. A Letter To All Affected: A Declaration From Dementia Itself

Dementia For Dummies: A Guide of Common Sense for Dummies

What is Dementia? If you had to tell someone who didn't know anything about it? What would you say?

Let's keep it simple, it's being trapped inside your mind,
The mind however feels like someone else's,
Total loss of thoughts, memories and reasoning,
respectfully.

It's feeling each nerve slowly crackle, fizzle and burn,
It erases the past, blurs the present and distorts real life,
Leaving loved ones lost in a bewildering maze,
You become a completely different person,
There's nothing predictable about it in any way.

Tasks once done without thought, now tangled and forgotten,
A jigsaw puzzle with one missing piece that eventually loses many more,

Finding familiarity in fake fantasies and feeling
unsafe in places I once loved,
Leaving gaps in the story, as I do in my head and
moves.

Dementia is basically becoming a brand-new
character,
Each day unpredictably problematic,
Physically and mentally different a lot,
An uncontrollable ever-changing decline.

Eventually they are no longer able to care for
themselves,
Calling us the wrong names and ages,
Unable to remember who we are,
Mind blank, bare and numb.

It's time blended together, days slipping away,
Familiar places and faces become strangers,
A rollercoaster of sickness, thrills and anxious
free-flying fate,
A plight of chaotic overload.

Dementia is a brain-distorting disorder,
Causing character dysfunction,
Any possible will or way.

A Letter

Dear un-dearest Dementia,
Regretfully and respectfully, I write to you again, withholding the power of my projection of pity and pain. Yet, I thank you for the challenge bestowed upon me, the character you have allowed me to become. For giving me family in work, uniting us deeply as I am educated on your end point. Thank you, as you believed yourself superior, but you have inadvertently made an inferior infectious interference. Thank you for letting me understand you, thank you for giving me something to fight for until the end of my days.

Let me be clear, the trauma you inflict on those entangled in your web must be shared, spoken out on and shut down to silence. You have become a toxic 'It Girl', intertwined maliciously in everyone's lives. We all know someone impacted by Dementia. Rest assured, we will fight against you with dying determination.

We all have, one common goal, one common good, one coming outcome!

We will continue to care compassionately and
personalise your plan.
We will continue to cheer proudly and push you
to live strong and full of will.
We will continue to celebrate and change your
definition.
We will continue to connect in community and
push back at every challenge you throw out.

Dementia, with my expertise, I've figured you
out,
Delirium can't deceive me,
Do you think I won't work daily to deliver
delight,
Dementia, we battle, never alone, till the last
kill!

I look forward to never thinking of you as
unbeatable. I am more grateful to say, our
relationship is now over. Your contribution to
anything other than research, is respectfully
declined and denied.

Please consider this as official documentation
terminating our bond of traumatic tribulations.
I would like to express gratitude for ridding you
from my life. Never to be spoken of again in
sorrow.

I wish you nothing but decomposition,
I wish you nothing but non-existence,
I wish you endless failure of fate,
I wish you no thanks or success.

Respectfully, I decline to acknowledge you any
further,

Unkind Regards,

"Someone who helps people to defeat you every
day".

We're All In This Together

Chapter 3: Can You Be Fully Represented
Through Me? - A Dementia Carer/Support
Worker's View

In the end, all we have, is love, memories, and
helping hands.
We're all in this together, we all think and feel
the same.
We're all in this together, the highs, the lows, the
joy, and the pain.

Although for all of us it's different, it's also
much the same.
We all go through a process of understanding,
confusion, and fighting til the last day.

From the very beginning, we hold the person
that has been.
Forever sticking together, bonding through
traumatic unity.
Giving all we've got, for the best chances and
opportunities.

A patient, loved one, or carer, all equally
involved and important.

The person-centred care plan, impossible
without all our voices shared.
Care is from the heart, the mind, lived
experience, something everyone can do, just by
listening.

In the end, all we have, is love, memories, and
helping hands.
We're all in this together, we all think and feel
the same.
We're all in this together, the highs, the lows, the
joy, and the pain.

The process doesn't get clearer, in fact more
challenging each day.
Denial, anger, bargaining, acceptance, waves of
depression constantly swaying through my
brain.

Throughout the middle of the process, we make
the most of what we've got.
Continuing to learn together, finding new ways
to adapt.
Struggling collectively, overcoming obstacles,
twists and turns.

Crucial are the relationships, routines, and
strength of character to cope.

A never-ending beautifully cruel cycle, conflict
embedded in rules that can't be broken.
The care is interchangeable, yet consistency is
the key.

In the end, all we have, is love, memories, and
helping hands.
We're all in this together, we all think and feel
the same.
We're all in this together, the highs, the lows, the
joy, and the pain.

There comes a time, to face the avoided and
dreaded truth, deciding on death, final wishes,
last requests and personal views.
One of the hardest stages of the process,
acceptance and grief fully kicking in.
Ticking clocks, daily panic attacks, wondering
when it will be our last day.

Facing the end of the process, is daunting,
scarring, but often a relief.
The loved one so lost in suffering, finally able to
rest in peace.
Overwhelming clouds of emotional darkness,
yet bright future visions of contentment and
feeling free.

All involved tightly woven together, resting our
heads on each other's shoulders.
A confusing feeling of guilt and regret, and
numbness identifies with me.
The times, and experience will never be
forgotten, it's forever engraved in our brains.

In the end, all we have, is love, memories, and
helping hands.
We're all in this together, we all think and feel
the same.
We're all in this together, the highs, the lows, the
joy, and the pain.

In the end all that matters is who we have not
what,
We all have mutual understanding, respect,
admiration, praise, and physical outburn.
We all sink or float as a whole, becoming one
for all and all for one.